The Return of the Bees

By
Marianne Betterly

BLUE LIGHT PRESS ◆ 1ST WORLD PUBLISHING

1ST WORLD
PUBLISHING

SAN FRANCISCO ◆ FAIRFIELD ◆ DELHI

The Return of the Bees

Copyright ©2016 by Marianne Betterly

1st World Library
PO Box 2211
Fairfield, IA 52556
www.1stworldpublishing.com
Email: worldlibrary@lisco.com

Blue Light Press
www.bluelightpress.com
Email: bluelightpress@aol.com

Book & Cover Design
Melanie Gendron
www.melaniegendron.com

First Edition

Library of Congress Control Number: 2016908220

ISBN 9781421837567

To Rick and Jack

Table of Contents

Boudhanath Wish

Goodnight

Haunted

Recycling

Stardust

Boudhanath Wish

Angels

Some say they are watching,
whispering answers,
helping find lost socks, wallets, hope.

They sit in trees,
on roof tops,
ride waves at the beach.

In every room, right now
one is standing next to you
on the left or maybe
the right.

No golden trumpets
no white robes
no wings.

Just minor miracles —
the perfect word,
a light bulb that flickers when you say his name,
a scarlet blossom on your morning walk
when you felt
the only color left
was black.

All for You, Nancy Drew

Nancy Drew,
my spirit guide
to the lilac garden beneath crumbling walls,
a clue
to the ticking clock
we choose not to hear
but know is there
each second pushing us closer
to discover the underside of what we fear.

Because of you
I am a street detective
recording whispers, the hidden kiss,
the sideways glances, the sighs
of the lost, lost in thought, the moments almost missed,
the lovers who breathe each other's air,
The cry of the fifteen year old
who sucks tears dry.

You helped me find
hidden staircases
inside a train ride
after sunrise lights those who wake
to cardboard walls and pigeon fluff.
I wander the empty alleys
as the first crane is rising
past tagged walls and broken locks
where last night furries danced like rabbit and fox.

Despite your change from flip to shag,
blond to Titian gold,
I can still find you, Nancy Drew,
In papers crumpled, letters lost,
with flashlight, keen sight, insight,
keys to preteen,
you helped unlock

and showed me
where to look for pursed lips, purple eyelashes,
gold glint inside a perfect smile,
my eyes wider with each clue
in the yellow bound mysteries
I could solve
over and over
with every turn of page and path,
a hideaway from jeers and sneers
in the training bra years.

Because of you, Nancy Drew
I am unafraid of a snapped twig in the night
or coyote howl.
With probing eyes
I seek the shadows —
for that is where the answers lie.

Finding Yusef

Philadelphia, 1972

Another sip of borrowed brandy,
hitch to a club
in the Philly slums
to see him —
modern Pan,
watch his fingers fly,
lips blow.
You can't get that from a record.

Outside,
hours before opening,
my long hair flashes teen innocence,
no fake ID,
no easy passage.

In front of Rizzo's Liquors
I pick up an old guy,
maybe forty-five,
gray hair,
wrinkled corduroy jacket,
the window of dusty bottles of Bali Hai
reflects his laugh lines, soft,
like rays of the sun.

Sure, if you buy my ticket.

Glasses clink with ice and booze,
smoky,
dark faces look
through him, at me,
try to keep my smile
in my eyes.

Yusef appears
playing two flutes at once, sweet,
tooting scales —
'Stay with Me' takes me higher
than the Acapulco gold I have in my purse.
He is my Orpheus.
I stay for the second set
into early morning,
too late to bus home.

Inside Jim's residence hotel —
mottled walls
smell of spilled whiskey and wine, puke,
cracked sink in the corner,
bathroom down the hall.
I rest on his gray mattress
bird flutter
heart.

He doesn't mind that I wear my clothes to bed.
This was the best night I've had in years,
he whispers
then hugs me with vodka breath,
long and hard,
before snores and twitch.
Awake all night,
I close my eyes when he gets up and
pisses in the sink.

No matter,
still high on a thousand
notes of flute.

A Tincture of Words

Poetry is a tincture of words.
One drop
drapes gray sky
in persimmon red
dripping with juices
ready to be licked.

Another drop
transmits love
deep as mother-and-son bonds
braided into a blue and green lanyard
at summer camp.
It paints Elizabethan passion
in sonnets' soft
metered kiss.

A poem
whispered in the wind
blows around the earth.
Each syllable
floats from London to L.A.
over Tokyo, Zanzibar
in electronic bits or
scratched on yellowed paper,
painted on walls,
repeated, chanted,
clapped to in church,
memorized,
interpreted,
absorbed,

transformed,
devoured.

Sacred syllables vibrate
through prayer flags
hung from mountain *stupas,*
hilltop homes,
bless the knowing
and unknown,
the wind horses grant wishes
to those below.
One droplet
becomes shimmers
of dawn light
through blood orange coral reefs
as thousands of silver striped fish
watch the sun burst
from the depths of the Caribbean sea.

One phrase becomes an introduction,
a kiss, a night of laughter,
future imagined in rhyme,
a best friend, a husband,
a father, a son.

One poem colors
a watery planet called Earth
aqua and white,
viewed from Apollo Eleven,
a speck,
a universe.

Mo

He sat in a white room, alone,
on a bed surrounded by
windows to the Bay.

His bald head matched Rick's —
their smiles reflected a twenty year bond as
teacher-student, director-subject, dharma friends,
as we huddled at his feet.

He fingered his prayer beads when
I asked my first question,

Should we go to Nepal now or next year?

No one spoke of the tumors
multiplying in Rick's liver,
but after the lama threw his mala,
twirled and tossed on the bed
three times:

Either is fine.

History Lesson

Blow drying my hair at the club,
I see Nefertiti pulling her black hair back,
flat against her head,
showing her long neck,
perfect Egyptian profile.
She dabs makeup under kohl black eyes,
adds a hair attachment,
covers it with an African scarf.

A geisha walks by in a tiny towel,
blossom mouth smiling,
no tattoos of dragons or orchids on her soft skin,
smooth, unmarked by moles or painted patterns.

A Spanish flamenco dancer kisses the mirror
as she layers lipstick, bright red
with painter's brush
before slipping on a black lace dress and white tennis shoes.

Several aging Chinese princesses giggle past
in skin-tight blue spandex
ready to Spin.

Marilyn, an exotic Asian queen,
did not come today.
She moves with grace and quiet beauty,
dances salsa in little black shorts and mini top,
exposes a flat naval we all wish we had.

Heather, a high-court courtesan, passes me
in her latest chartreuse top, tight white pants, gold lamé shoes.
After hip hop, she is ready to ascend the high rise.

The only real blond in the dressing room,
I am a Viking from ice fields, Queen of Snow,
who must apply brown to blond lash and brows,
sunscreen to white nose, cheeks and chin
before walking outside in the Oakland sun,
leaving centuries of
naked history
behind.

Boudhanath Wish

As he runs up the *stupa's* steps
monkey speed,
I worry he might fall,
but instead of chasing my son,
I fumble with my camera.

The blue eyes of Buddha,
eyes unlike any other,
are watching him from above.
I want to remember the moment —
our eight-year-old wild child running
through the streets of Kathmandu,
his father, chemo-bald,
smiling.

A rainbow of prayer flags flutter above us,
sending wind horse blessings to change bad luck to good.

Beneath Buddha's eyes
we buy a wooden cage of finches,
a Buddhist custom to release the birds,
granting wishes and compassion to all beings.

Back at Hotel Vajra
my son opens the cage door,
closes his eyes,
whispers his wish.

The birds become
dots in the evening sky.

Navajo Man

His dented door screeches shut.
The pickup bumps up and down
as we travel the sunburned land
over yellowed grass, lumps of hills.
Dirt road behind us shimmers, then evaporates,
like coyotes at dusk.

He stretches silence across
cactus, boulders, sage brush
despite my talk of Anasazi caves,
Navajo sand paintings, Tibetan *mandalas*.

No glance, no nod
as we drive zigzags
through Arizona summer heat.

Hundreds of potholes later
we stand on a windy cliff,
watch the vastness blow
down the canyon
to tomorrow.

He points in the four directions —
finally he speaks:
This is my land, Navajo land.
We will fight
for our earth.

Thunder cracks like Cavalry rifles.
We both look up:
a bear scrambles in a passing cloud
while wind hisses like a snake
calling out to the god of rain.

Bridge to Junbesi

No rope rail
nothing to hold
on my way to the other side,
only spray and splash,
a thirty foot plank over wild torrents.
My heart throbs in my throat.

Rick hikes with liver lesions spreading
thoughts of endings and
future journeys missed.
His mantras murmured past
mani walls won't stop
his fear.

Our son's stomach rising like bread,
pain of amoeba.
Was it the ice cream?
No doctor for a hundred miles,
my stomach hurts to watch him cry.

One bridge to cross
extending over the dragon river.
Makeshift logs roped, knotted this morning
after the bridge washed
downstream.

Death swirls in endless icy water
from Everest's crags and clefts
cascading down to India
where hundreds drown every year.

On the Junbesi side, villagers and Lama
wait for us with *khatas* and tea,
send a Sherpa with rope
in case someone falls in.

If we make it across this river —
can we cross the next bridge?

I put one foot out,
whispering prayers,
holding nothing
but my breath.

Tale of the Cicada

"When we try to pick out anything by itself,
we find it hitched to everything else in the Universe."
— John Muir

The party was just beginning
when I split a tab with Chucky.
A crowd gathered to watch
his cupped hands open,
as he slowly revealed a Cretaceous creature,
insouciant sleeper,
burrowed for a decade
waiting
to rise like a saint,
send sound waves
into the Andromeda night

He opened his hands,
whispered incantations,
as the cicada grew larger
than my brother's yellow VW bug,
its wild eyes rolling,
wings fluttering faster
than a helicopter's twirl
with a buzz so loud
it cracked the sky.
A thousand stars sprinkled
on the grass.

My eyes became
singing bowls.
I fell into a web that connected us all,

floated in prehistoric sound
while the bug loomed large,
filling the backyard
with waves of rattled song.

The threads still glimmer over
Berkeley and the Bay,
connecting sky to earth,
me to you,
in arachnoid space.

Goodnight

Goodnight

He is still,
eyes meeting mine,
as Joshua Redmond's sax
blows soft sad notes

in our bedroom on Sunday night,
heat still lingering
in the sun porch
overlooking
haze on the bay.

Should be time for our favorite show
or ice cream and syrup with Jack
before a goodnight book
and hug.

Instead I am kissing him
goodbye
as his look goes deep inside
and his inhale
isn't followed by another
breath.

I hold his hand
since he can't hold mine,
a white circle
in the center of his palm
grows larger
until his hand is a cold glove
and he
is
memory.

Light Bulbs

Five light bulbs
popped tonight.

The last time that happened
our house was filled with people,
air was thick with grief,
the day after
Rick died.

Each time I said his name
lamps flickered and dimmed,
the fax machine fizzled,
phone battery died,
computer crashed,
my home blackened,
without electricity.
Confused,
I fumbled to find fuses
in the dark
without my husband.

He would have known
how to turn the lights on.

Maybe Rick wanted our house
silent,
cut off from sound and light,
so I could feel him
privately
before returning to my routines
in a new world without him.

Maybe he was lingering
in the dark,
waiting, watching.

He had filled our house
with a thespian voice.
His laughter spilled onto the street
spouting Elizabethan sonnets,
chanting Tibetan mantras,
telling me he loved me.
Now a shadow,
scent of Bel Ami,
stack of fedoras,
photo of him smiling,
a light that burnt out.

Sometimes I feel him late at night,
in a dream or
when a sound
wakes me
in the hour of the wolf.

We are alone,
in altered states,
without baggage
of bodies.

I miss his touch.

Our son yells,
Mom, we need to change
the light bulbs!

Time to turn on
the lights.

644 Cranes

for Sadako Sasaki (1943-1955)
A Japanese legend states if you fold 1000 cranes,
your wish is granted.

She didn't plan to fly
out the window
when the bomb burst
over Misasa Bridge

on winds of poisoned atoms,
scorching fire,
in the flash
that branded earth and sky.

August's green gone,
the city,
black and white rubble,
nothing left but
mutant seeds
in our memory,
her blood.

The cranes she folded
from candy wrappers,
borrowed envelopes
hospital trash —
each one creased, bent,
shaped into
hope
for another day,
another breath.

If only she could make
1,000
she might fly
out of the cancer ward.

My Son is an Artist, Too

for Antonio Ramos (1988 - 2015),
killed on West St, Oakland, while painting a Super Heroes mural

Like you, my son is an artist.
He transforms sloths and toilets, punk singers and Grandma
into paintings on my wall.

Like you, he lived in Oakland,
roamed the same routes,
avoided the same bumps and dives,
the shifty-eyed druggies, the abandoned mattresses,
the women lingering on the corner a little too long.

And now you both have left —
Jack moved after his roommate was pistol-whipped,
then robbed of wallet, laptop, phone in front of their house.
You left when a bullet silenced you
as you painted a peace mural
of urban heroes and transformation.

I often journeyed deep in the same war zone
to pick up my son.
This time I took a detour to see your mural,
now surrounded by a crumbling shrine:
a wilting wreath, dirty teddy bears, a shrouded head.
I walked the sidewalk between rows of *veladora* candles
and the mural of hope,
a bouquet of paint brushes and half-used spray cans.

In the underpass, the dead zone,
the space of darkness, crime, crack heads —

your artwork colors the wall with a Madonna blessing, doves
and whispered wishes that fly toward heaven.

My son is an artist, too.
He left West Oakland before it was too late —
the same month you became a hero,
trying to transform violence with Art,
but even Superman is not strong enough
to stop every bullet.

We Widows

We widows
walk the world
hidden in the crowd.
Some wear white,
others black.

Golden band on finger,
turned like a prayer wheel
spinning memories
of his voice —
a ghost hand
presses fingers
like a flower under glass,
mementos sealed
in Snow White's tomb.

Indian widows burn
their gold and red saris.
Sometimes they jump in,
swimming in flames,
red vermillion gone
from world drained of color.

All that remains —
my wedding vows,
musky sport coat,
a box of yellowed papers,
cards hidden in sock drawer
I will always love you

wedding kimono folded
like a paper doll,
white album
stuffed with faded smiles,
a dried red rose.

We widows
walk the world
hidden in the crowd.
Some wear black,
others white,
alone.

Green

For Anna Katherine Greene, my great-great aunt, a mystery writer

I have been searching for green
in the bay tree, the camellias blooming, the magnolia,
a leaf of the lemon tree,
the green page of the Chronicle newspaper,
a stamp from Nepal,
on my cashmere sweater between threads of aqua and cream

but I can't find it —
the right green
not evergreen, mint green, olive green
not the perky wake-me-up shocking green
I use for a fruit bowl
or the dull green of soldiers ready to fly to Afghanistan

not Kermit or lime or pippin —
none of these are right.
I need a mysterious green
one that shape-shifts
sometimes passes for yellow
one that lives behind the retina,
one that screams,
then gets lost down the Amazon
in the jungles of Mato Grosso,

a green that can cover the blood on
the Sword of Damocles,
a green that can fill the sky,
a green that will be remembered
for centuries
after your books are dust.

Prayer to Ma'at

"as above, so below"

Ma'at doesn't smile on bullets and bombs,
bleeding bodies,
bitter blue scarabs lost in broken rock,
pieces of pyramid hurled
in a shower of blood.

Did they forget to weigh their hearts
against the feather of truth?

All I see are crowds of angry men,
shooting and shouting
but sanguine sandstorms
eventually
die with the wind,

letting hope rise
like incantations
to awaken the living.

Rabbits Run

They multiply in the shadows,
hop on every stitch of lawn until
soft fur and balls of white cover mown grass,
turn plots of green into
a tumultuous
river of gray.

The rabbit rave repeats each night
in a soft jumble of leaps,
a silent ballet of frenzied cottontails
jump to beats
heard only by soft rabbit ears.

But when the moon rises,
lighting the lapidarian dance,
coyotes join in,
changing the music to
tango abrazo,
close embrace.

Musings in the Morning

Wet shrouds of fog float in winter sky
Why didn't I cry when he left me?

The train car is full of silent people with raucous thoughts.
Is unemployment a passport to the world?

100 decibel screech as we break at Ashby.
I miss my father's puns.

Sunrise is losing its battle with fog.
Will my 19 year old son ever go to bed before 5AM?

Tattoos hibernate in winter, not one in sight.
Should I see my mother before she gets worse?

Finally a hint of gold between Oakland's skyscrapers.
Goodbye is never enough.

Haunted

The Return of the Bees

Ancient Greeks believed that bees carry souls of the dead.

The bees arrived before dinner,
while we were toasting my husband
with champagne,
sixth anniversary of his passage.

They darkened the sky
in a cyclone,
filling my backyard bay tree,
buzzing louder than a leaf blower
or my son's electric guitar,
thousands of tiny bodies,
golden
in the late afternoon sun.

I was not afraid when
a few bees flew in my kitchen window,
stuck to the wall, quietly watching me.
Honey bees,
dancing pollinators,
weaving in the wind,
left their hive
to follow a new queen,
start a new life.

A miracle,
like the first swarm that appeared in my yard
after Buddhist prayers
for Rick's bardo,
when a buzzing ball of bees

hung like a dark shadow
under a branch of liquid amber,
humming for a week outside our bedroom window,
pollinating my plants,
funeral flowers still fresh.
Both times they disappeared before dawn,
filtering through ancient redwoods,
blending with the stars,
a swarm of souls
flying into the night.

Ghost Veils

Spanish moss drips
from oak and elm,
hangs like gray veils
on a ghost bride.

Wind moans
through the branches
while they cry.

Some say spirits
live in trees.

I think the moss
mourns young brides
who lost their life
before their innocence,
like the orange blossom bride
buried in her wedding dress.

The gray moss wraps each tree in a web,
but unlike a victim,
the tree welcomes its invader
and wears the long, tangled threads
as if floating down the aisle,
while Carolina breezes swirl
its ancient silks,
antebellum lace.

Atlas in Shroud

How many suns and moons have passed
watching shadows shrink and grow?
Webs are woven where pupils go,
lips are silenced into stone.

Holes can never be filled
in this land of emptiness
but you remain,
without words or tears

to touch those who wander
gray days and sleepless nights
up the marbled steps
to your hollow watch.

Bokeh

Morning begins in pastel glow
slipping golden light
into dreams.

Eyelids flutter
as the haze of nocturne knocked out
by caws of crow and rumble of bus and stomach.

I reach for you
but find only air and lost hope
in my room of ghosts.

I hear whispering
perhaps a branch
brushing my wooden walls.

Neon numbers blink six twenty,
flash the day into focus.
Maybe today I'll write in Calliope's notebook,

capture the blur
before all that is left
is bird song.

Grandma Gone

Shreds of Kleenex form a trail from bathroom to bedroom.
Pill jars line the kitchen counter,
miracle vitamins to restore memory, Youth.
Boxes of Cindy Crawford cream arrive every week,
fill the bathroom shelves,
reduce wrinkles.
Stop the Clock.

She shuffles, sniffs,
a hump appeared sometime in the past few years.
She used to do New York Times crosswords,
complained if they were too easy.

But those puzzles are lost
under piles of old newspaper, unpaid bills,
unsent donations to the Cancer Society and Policemen's Funds.
The accordion files for mortgage,
insurance and taxes are filled with junk mail,
and hundreds of yellowed newspaper clippings about
Nazi concentration camps and survivor Jews
mixed with recipes for chicken cacciatore and artichoke soup.

Our last meal was at a restaurant in Berkeley
Does it have stairs?
I forgot the two steps up to the dining room,
she sighs after each step.

The supper begins with French fries, shared.
Jack doesn't order anything, eats only bread and fries.

Peter cleans his plate.
Grandma picks at her shrimp.
What is this? Did I order it?
Her strawberry shortcake,
dry, tasteless,
she devours with gusto.

No one mentions the afternoon flight
to the East Coast with Peter or
her future room in a place
that will never be Home.
When I kiss her goodbye
she gives me a look
I haven't seen since my child gazed up at me,
nestled in my arms.

Balinese Thunder

Thunder rolls across the temple tops,
rice paddies and coconut palm
birds echo
the cry of rain
in coo coo caw
and cock crow
a natural gamelan ringing
dark storm
about to strike.

You would have loved the green
in the air
the incense and flowers on every path,
every street a temple.

Ganesh watches through doorways
marigold mala bright
against moss trunk.

At tonight's ceremony to Vishnu,
in Pura Puseh, I will call to you
in your new body,
avatar between cloud and earth.

A blessing,
a gold and white plumeria,
a *Sarasvati* song.

His Brown Eyes Became Air

His brown eyes became air,
wind from the west,
no tracking, blinking, crying —
hands frozen,
laughter squeezed into an album,
extinguished
like the evening sun.

I asked him for a sign
on his return —
a wink or stare from a stroller,
a message in a new voice,
a familiar joke would do.

Only whispers in a dream —
his words float outside,
like the hummingbird at my window,
the spider dangling over my bed.

Ghosts I Have Met

When we bought *Ghosts I Have Met*,
at Moe's bookstore on Telegraph,
we giggled after reading the first page,
vowed to read one page aloud
every night before bed.

Not that we did.

I didn't know that in twelve years
I would be in bed, alone,
reading that book to you.

You entered the world
of mist and lights,
sudden breezes closing doors,
before I was ready
to say goodbye.

We still see each other in
shadows and dreams,
but bodies make things happen.

I understand the Buddhist phrase,
precious human body,
now that I no longer can touch your fingertips,
feel your naked chest against mine,
whisper in your ear,
hear you chuckle.

You cannot warm my pillow —
even if you heat my heart.

Maybe you can help me write
a new page about the otherworld —
where you go when you are not with me,
how it feels to pass through walls and mirrors,
become the wind,
float across the pale sky.

Haunted

I didn't pale
when a bottle of Pinot flew off the wine rack
while thinking
You would know what to drink.
I was unafraid when the lights dimmed
as I touched your favorite sheet,

but when your pith helmet fell
from the bookshelf at midnight,
hitting the floor with a bang,
as I cried

There's nothing anyone can do,
I just want my husband back!

I knew you were in the living room,
somewhere.

I hoped you heard me whisper
I like to know you are here,
but don't scare me again

When I opened your mail
the next day,
found a temporary membership card for you
from The Reincarnation Library,
good for 30 days,
non-transferable,
I laughed.

Now your messages are fewer,
more oblique.
Did you want me to find
the heart in my underwear drawer
on Valentine's Day?

Maybe you've moved on
to a new body without wrinkles,
worry,
cancer.

I asked a lama for advice
You can't hug water, light, wind.

Bird's Eye View

Yesterday was a day of crows
swooping cars and rooftops,
pecking at the dead in dirt,
they disappear in a murder of wings,
a black umbrella blown into the sky.

Could it be a sign
to speed up,
have another double latte,
turn up the music, Mr. Jones,
follow the internet path
from crow augury to animal totems,
cathedrals in France,
pause at Counting Crows,
seven for a secret never to be told.

Some birds fly so fast
you don't see their flight —
only a glimmer of hummingbird wing,
a flicker of finch.

I'd rather think it is a message to slow down,
count each feather,
smell the seed and worm on bird breath,
go eye to eye with a red-tailed hawk
atop an old Redwood
where the only rush —
a whoosh of Bay fog,
followed by
silence.

Recycling

Recycling

They are late today
screeching brakes outside my house,
a staccato of backup beeps,
cans rolling,
then grinding, mashing
as all our leftovers are taken away.

Tucked between the morning paper and empty envelopes —
a few of your unsent letters in
distinctive pen and dipped blue ink,
the curves of your Y and R
become your laughing eyes
across the breakfast table while
writing a card to a monk in Kathmandu
between sips of espresso and bites of cinnamon toast.

Your words now trucked
to a paper afterlife,
maybe compacted into a cube
or mixed with coffee grounds and egg shells.

I didn't toss them all,
made just enough space
for a few new cards in a different hand mingled with
photos of evening star cymbidiums,
Paris at dusk,
the Cartwheel Galaxy floating like a jelly fish,
and a wish or two.

Wood and Earth

You were a Zen temple
with a garden of raked sand,
ancient stone,
Buddha face in half smile.

I was a willow,
always bending,
green tears dripping in the wind.

You were cricket floors of dark wood
waiting for someone to creep in,
surprise you in a dream.

I was plum blossoms in Spring,
air with petal
pink rain,
floating for a day.

You echoed with chants,
koans emptied of purpose,
one vase waiting.

You were shoji screens
that filtered light but not the cold
of winter winds,
the frost before sunrise.

I was the mourning dove
that cooed on your roof

until a hawk swooped,
talons open.

You were the clay-tiled roof
heavy with snow,
in cold diamond light.

I was koi in the pond,
golden scales slipping
under and around,
an infinite loop,
going nowhere.

Steps and Bows in Tokyo

A day of a thousand steps
down subterranean stairs, bright tunnels, through snapping doors.
My teenage son and I sit silently on the subway
in a line of glazed Tokyo commuters
whose same shoes, soft thoughts, semi-closed lullaby eyes
make us feel like the strangers we are,
the only blonds on the train.
No one really stares but
the silence keeps getting louder
as I try to understand the metro map.
The only poster I can read has no words,
warns against speaking on cell phones,
how conversations might make a stranger cry.

We wander on narrow Harajuku streets
where girls wobble in three inch gladiator shoes,
pink maid frills, bright red hair,
boys cluster, hollow-cheek lean, jagged bangs
waterfall over their eyes,
a rich woman pushes a baby carriage —
inside: a Chihuahua dressed in pink ruffles and bows.

Night drops around us like a thunder burst.
We return to the alleyways of Asakusa mall, hungry for sushi —
this one has sushi on boats.
Thank god I can read *kanji* numbers.
Stacks of plates later
our bill is somehow less than dinner in Berkeley.

The mall is covered in pink paper *sakura*,
hundreds of stalls sell kimonos, cameras,
chopsticks, ceramic bowls.
I keep finding mementos I would have bought for him
if I weren't his widow.
A little past ten, most shops closed except for *pachinko*.
As we pass the sushi boat restaurant again,
the chef and two waitresses come outside,
bow to us as if honored guests.
We wave and when we turn the corner, look back —
a second bow, deeper,
warms me like a sip of *shochu* before goodnight.

Lost and Found

I stand alone
in a street full of cars
alone with a keyless key
my car gone,
an old blue Mazda parked
in its place.

Earlier, wrapped in Lexus leather,
I sang to surround-sound Sting
sequestered from clang of train,
strain of Friday deadlines,
chatter of children and chipmunk . . .

now solo
like a slip of paper floating
updraft
in a winter wind.

Could it be the creep of years
or distraction of tears
that blurs the cars, the street
into a Turner landscape?

Perhaps my car wandered
like my eight-year old son in Kathmandu,
discovered later
draped in a Burmese Python,
tooting flute to a cobra,
between snake charmers

in Dunbar Square.
The crowd amazed at the small blond child
unafraid of slithering snakes.

Did a thief hotwire my car
for a joy ride through Oakland's back streets?

I'm not ready to call 911, a friend or Uber
to help me home.

I walk the other direction —
down another block,
find my car,
parked,
where it always was,
waiting,

the way my son waited for me
when I lost him in Glasgow
among Scottish Sunday shoppers.

After hunting miles of crowded cobblestone streets
I returned to the spot he disappeared
to find him standing there,
bored,
and unlike me,
un-lost.

Teotihuacan Stairway

Rustle of phantom reeds,
howls of jaguar, hawk, wolf,
bound enemies, Mayan ghosts,
bone chips of the dead,
mingle with obsidian knives
inside pyramid walls.

Climbing stone ladder steps,
steep stairway
up pyramid of the moon,
getting closer to the gods,
final stop on the Avenue of the Dead.
Panting in the hot breeze,
only a few more crumbling steps
to reach the first level
for a perfect view of sun pyramid,
taller than the moon,
covered with ant people,
peak seekers with strong legs and hearts,
compelled to reach the top for their one-minute photo,
like those on Everest or Kilimanjaro,
who quickly descend,
never to return.

I prefer the plumed serpent stone,
butterfly frescoes,
a moment alone
in silent prayer
for those who died where I stand.

How many took their final breath on these stairs?

My heart beats like
hummingbird wings,
tzunuum.

Mexican clouds blow through me.
It's always harder going down.

Spirits in Our Machines

Invisible, they live within your TV,
smart phone, car, laptop,
even in your blender and coffee grinder.

Humming a haunting echo,
pulsing with electrode energy,
they know your coffee and Facebook addictions,
your passions at midnight.
They've been with you when you were drunk,
watched you cry for your lost husband,
distracted you when you were sick
with Homeland and True Detective,
showed you Sufis twirling when you were too tired to spin,
filled the screen with Salgado's black and white photos
of battle-torn bodies,
made your suffering a speck of dust.

So why are you surprised
when they rebel,
refuse to go to the recycling bin?
They prefer to live in your garage or pocket,
want to listen to laughter in the living room,
do not want to die in a garbage heap.

They seem to read your mind
when you are packing them for electronic waste:
the smart phone won't shut down,
the Audi won't start
when about to hand the keys at Pick 'n Pull.

Your PC has one last gasp
after the blue screen of death and disk drive screech.
It reboots to reveal
a checkerboard of ghosts.

Bite

Your morning oracle
promises to promote
the perfect pout,
preferred angles of neck and chin —
for glances, whispers, midnights

then she arrives . . .

her skin,
river stone smooth
with a smile of pearls.
Her emerald eyes light up
under lashes that curl
toward the rising sun.

You are buried
under bandaged hope,
scorched history
of never-afters.

You can't avoid
the highway veins, the burns, the peels,
the spots that never disappear

so you brush your newly blackened hair,
scarlet gloss your lips,
dangle diamonds from both lobes —
hide the wrinkles, creases, lumps
under chiffon and silk

but somehow
you are still invisible as the wind
while she dances with birds and words,
sings of first times,
exhales teen freshness,
hungry for love to appear
in her thicket of dreams.

So you hand her an apple
seeped in curiosity,
filled with curse,
dipped in red lacquer
deeper than a goodbye kiss.

The Dark Side of the Rainbow

Everyone loved her heels —
they were sexy,
sparkled like the fourth of July
three inches of spike —
and the way she swayed her hips
when she showed them off
walking like a runway model
in skintight Armanis,
that kissed her curves,
made men into animals,
or clowns or dwarves —
one lost his heart.

Rumor had it she
found them on a homeless woman,
dead,
and pulled them off the corpse,
tried them on and
strutted into the night.

A video of her went viral,
two minutes on YouTube ending with clicked heels,
her trademark
like Michael's moonwalk.

Other rumors she never denied —
she hated monkeys and men in uniforms
and was in a lawsuit with the dead girl's sister,
a real witch,

who claimed the shoes were hers,
and demanded their return,
muttering murder

but Dorothy just said *no, I'm innocent*
while she twirled her pigtails
like a Japanese Lolita,
flashing sparkling pumps and polished teeth

so when she left town in a hurry,
flying high as a balloon,
no one was surprised
that she skipped out
with the rubies.

My Scars are My Tattoos

Some ink themselves
with kanji or Tibetan
for dharma, hell —
their fire dragons fly,
birds and words circle biceps and thighs,
covered in a maze of meanings,
faces of heroes, skulls and roses,
red riding hood, a devil kiss

My arms are white,
flecked with freckles,
a mole or two.

My scars are my tattoos.

I don't want to line my lips in eternal pink,
or replace brows with a permanent
thin black line
I want to erase spots from my skin,
remove all patterns
and dots.

I wear knife wounds,
straight lines
on belly, face, arm,
as permanent medals
of victory over death.

My scars are my tattoos

I want to become blindingly white,
not a trace
or footstep marking time.

Why ink your skin
with a name, face or flower,
a constant memory
some day you may want to forget

I don't want
needled reminders
of passing passion.

Your smile is embedded
on my wall of faces,
no inked portrait could ever
replace …

My scars are my tattoos.

Skin Writing

He unfurls me like a frond
uncoils my fingers
toes
unrolls both legs
until open to the sky.

He begins
in Celtic circles
he writes across my back,
a temporary tattoo of red words
that linger on skin.

I want to read them
but cannot see,
wrap him in
green tendrils
before all traces
of fingertips and kiss
slowly shrink

and when I curl my arms, legs
back into a bud
his words are gone,

leaving a tingling
like poison ivy
before the first
scratch.

Stardust

Coffee Augury

How long, I wonder,
as I stand in line —
ten cappuccinos and lattes
ahead of me.

I'm behind a blue jeans couple from the Mission,
twentyish,
both slim hipsters.
He has a star tattoo under his right ear —
his other tattoos are hidden today.

His unshaved face is soft.
She keeps touching him,
twirling around him like ivy,
then unwraps her arms
to push him forward,
one foot closer to java.
Their fingers entwine.
He kisses her forehead with a half-smile,
looking outside
at the mist rising over Mint Plaza.

He yields to her whispers.
Their lips touch five times
before ordering
lattes and brioche
then disappear onto stools against
the wall of windows.

Donovan sighs
wear your love like heaven …
My turn at the register.

La Marzocco espresso machine
hisses, gurgles,
coffee grinder infuses
Indonesia into the room.

The barista rings up my Blue Bottle cappuccino,
signs my coffee with a heart.
The milk foam art floats
in the center of my cup,
perfect
like the full moon.

Sugar crystals sink slowly as I stir.
The heart becomes a face —
my daily oracle.

I'll meet someone soon.

I sip the prophecy,
swallow slowly.
Make it come true.

Hot Kisses

The lure of slip and slide
hot kisses at midnight
panties lost in tangled sheets

linger in unmarked time,
avoid worry lines
that disturb dreams to come.

Only the living feel
the touch of skin to skin,
prickling spine and thigh
as fingertips follow curves into a crevasse,

spelunk the dark
explore stalagmites
as they arise

until the morning light
awakens the dreamer
out of haze and daze
into lips whispering
half-truths,
half-lies.

Altar

It was his altar.

Buddhist art,
sacred relics from trips to Tibet and Kathmandu,
Kyoto, streets of Berkeley.
He was a treasure hunter, a collector —
his altar overflowed.

In the center, a *thangka* painting of Lord of the Dance
stared into the living room with three eyes,
his consort wrapped in tantric embrace.
The medicine Buddha, golden
but for lapis lazuli hair,
blessed the house,
left hand cradling a bowl of nectar,
the other held a healing sprig.
The statue reflected morning light,
protected him in his prayers
to heal the cancer
eating his body
from bladder to kidney,
slowly spreading like a drop of red
ink in a pool of white.

I never polished the silver bowls
filled with Tibetan *dzi* beads,
coral, turquoise, rice.
I didn't rearrange Tibetan texts piled on the bottom shelf,
sacred poems and mantras,

red cloth cover faded with time and touch,
I didn't move the Nepali incense, bundles
in a wooden incense box,
the carved lions keeping negative spirits away.
I didn't dust the crystals, *dorjes*,
photos of the Dalai Lama, Trulshig and Dujom Rimpoche.
I never held the skull cup
or pressed my lips to the trumpet
made of bone.

It was his altar.

His tiny boxes of *ratna samphel*,
precious pills wrapped in paper —
medicine from the Dalai Lama's doctor,
filled with special herbs and blessings
to cure malignant thoughts.
They kept him alive after his liver shut down,
until all he could do was
blink his eyes.

Years later
when I could see again,
I noticed cobwebs on the altar.
I dusted the Buddhas,
swept the rice that covered one shelf,
placed the texts in a neat pile,
gathered the incense, scattered and broken.
I burned three sticks for him, one for me,
inhaled the musky scent of monasteries and meditation,
for our life together.

It is my altar.

Homage to the High Rise

As fog lifts
over dormant alleys and the seven hills,
I watch your silver and copper helmets
reflect the morning rays
that pierce San Francisco skyline's jagged juts
in razor cuts
of light.

I cannot touch your denim overalls
but watch you
five stories high:
the boot shuffle,
the orange sparks
as they fly
in a waterfall of fire
onto damp gray sidewalk
and homeless piss.

I want to shout hello but no one will hear
While the cement truck rolls --
pouring lumpy lava
into giant squares,
to be flattened and smoothed
into a permanent slab
to cradle a thousand office souls.

Decades ago
you would wolf whistle
from girders or backhoe,

behind a cyclone fence,
at any mini skirt in high heels
clipping down Mission
while Indian summer unrolled its heat.
How I blushed
at your hunger
for naked legs and soft teen lips.

Now I sip my Blue Bottle coffee,
hum to the sound
of new worlds rising —
watch you dig pits
from blueprints of pipe and wire,
meld metal mountains.

I walk beneath the red crane,
larger than King Kong,
as you disappear inside,
grab its throttle,
twist and turn,
lift copper-colored girders into the clouds.

Nothing can quite capture
the morning razzle, the crunch,
the sudden jets of hot steam,
the slow rise
of the high rise.

Writing Group

We expose our bald spots, surgery scars,
unread letters in a cardboard box,
tattoos of scorpions, stars, Madonna dethroned,
postulate the purpose of a penis in a painting.

We tweak commas, endings, rework titles
to punch, grab and shock,
sooth and coddle, fondle and cut
poems about freshly mowed grass, decaying bodies.

We circumambulate cancer in Kathmandu,
rest on Pennsylvanian porches,
smell the coal burn, remember forbidden kisses,
taste the juicy fruit tongue.

We meet hobos wearing top hats who dig holes,
dog-saints and praying mantis who watch while
we flaunt and fawn, paint and form
paragraphs that punch out teeth and lights.

We escape from brown bears and phone calls from phonies,
explore crystal caves and our future without oil.
We wear gowns to balls and hospital wards,
meet ghosts of husband, father, mother, unborn son.

We make love with firecracker syntax,
kill pain with spicy adjectives and silky verbs.
We blow a parting kiss to our past lives
again and again in our circle of words.

We weep at moments missed
for telling the truth about a lie.
We edit syllables for staccato,
add spaces and breaks to breathe.

We listen to secrets inside sonnets
try not to drown in detritus, plastic or paper,
swirl in oceans deeper than his kiss,
mirror our mother's smile in our children.

We strip down to bone, shed shadows,
cover nakedness in another wellspring of words
while we comment, extract, interpret,
embrace, swallow, shape-shift,
absorb.

To My Son

in memory of his father

You never asked
where he went
after his last breath,
as you watched
white dots
on each palm
grow larger
until his hands were
forever frozen —

never wondered about heaven,
only hell,
no angel wings
or spirits that glimmer.
The door was not shut
by a ghost,
just the wind.

Your magic ring had failed
no matter how often you'd rubbed it.
You stopped searching for the first evening star
since wishes never came true.

You never said goodbye
because you couldn't bear him to leave

and even now, you can't see him
though he is there,
in the mirror,
staring back.

Asakusa Geisha

Her ghost-white profile,
onyx hair,
tiny red lips
flashed
like mid-Summer lightning
in Asakusa
covered mall.

Who knows
where she is headed,
kimono tight,
forcing
tiny cocoon steps
in wooden sandals
white socks.

I watch her
plum-red obi
sway
on the back of
her oyster silk
kimono,
chrysanthemums
twisting with each step,
the folded package
shrinks as she
blends
into pulsing
neon Edo,

last hour of shopping
at post-*sakura* dusk.

She weaves through
minivans and shops selling
Chanel purses,
bins of lighters
shaped into frogs
and fans.

The crowd opens
like bamboo bending
in gentle wind
as she floats by.

I follow her past
plastic sushi and ramen bowls
behind glass,
until we reach
racks of
used kimonos for sale,
27,000 yen.

How much
for her *shamisen*
song?

I Want to Dance

I want to dance like Ginger,
swirling with Fred
as if our feet
were stitched together,
twirling madly
across the white gazebo,
safe from sudden downpour
but not from
each other.

I want to dance like Fred,
buffed black shoes
tapping lullabies
on cigarette sand
erasing midnight banter
with sprinkles of
happily ever after.

I want to dance like Cyd,
long legs wrapped tight
as a Japanese gift box,
spring open, twirling,
entwine men in boa embrace,
ready to squeeze and swallow.

I want to dance like Michael,
zombie-jerking between gravestones
moonwalking across Hollywood,
spinning for Billie Jean

and every kid in high tops —
rubber legs and arms,
tennis shoe toes en pointe
smiling through the flames.

I want to dance like Gene,
splashing in puddles
tapping black umbrella
air shoes leaping on lampposts
heel clicking
in wet song.

I want to dance like the Jets,
kickbox ballet across
empty basketball courts,
finger snapping
through graffiti alleys
on the West Side,
up wire fences,
swimming in heavy air,
floating down into the shadows
between love and death.

Stardust

Funeral procession in Ubud, Bali 2013

Not just the ceremonial pomp —
four hundred men in batik sarongs,
Western t-shirts, naked feet
spin a fifty-foot tower.

Ferocious demons blur
in a red haze.
A royal corpse precarious on the top,
sways in the ominous dark clouds.

The crowd presses their hands together,
wai,
each holds incense, pink flowers.
A shock of color as orange, black, purple Balinese sarongs
merge like bees in a swarm.

It was no surprise to the priests
when the heaviness of the sky
opens and torrents begin to fall on the bull and dragon,
maiden and prince, and corpse tower
while musicians bang drums,
women wail on their way to the cremation.

The angry clouds pour for hours.
Western women scale walls
to avoid the flood.
We shelter under the pavilion,
the death parade, long gone,
a memory in the sheets of rain.

Later when I arrive at the cremation,
a small sliver of blue appears between black cumulus.
The deluge, now mist as
the odor of fire fills Ubud.
The royal body already inside the burning bull,
lost in wild flames.

I circumambulate the crumbling tower,
recall the day
I watched your body burn,
how we covered you with paper mementos,
Buddhist amulets, a final kiss.

A box of ashes, stardust.

The children tear the demon eyes and smiles off the tower,
carry the shreds as souvenirs.

Suddenly the sun pierces the sky,
lighting puddles,
placing halos on tree tops,
brilliance.

Acknowledgements

Poetry has always been part of my life from early childhood, writing poems about imaginary cats to college heartache-and-soul poems. More recently, thanks to Linda Watanabe McFerrin and her writing classes, I began my journey as a poet: writing regularly about life in the Bay Area, motherhood and sadly, about widowhood. This book would never have been possible without her encouragement and support as well as the other writing groups that I have joined over the past decade. I am indebted to Judy Bebelaar, Tom Centolella, Gail and Charles Entrekin and their group including Demian, Grace, Judy and Antoinette, the Women's Poetry Potluck Salon, Jannie Dresser, and my own group, The Cheyannas: Alice Friedemann, Diane Richwine, Sierra Crawford, Victoria LaFond and Elaine Bond. Also special thanks to Diane Frank for helping me get this book to print. Finally I want to give a huge thank you to Barbara Quick, Jeanne Wagner and Shela Ray for editing my manuscript. In addition I want to thank Jeff Greenwald, Alice F. and Shela R. and my son, Jack, for supporting me in ways they will never know or understand. Sometimes just listening to a new poem, showing up to a reading, being there... that's what it is all about. I could not have done it without them.

I want to thank the following anthologies, magazines and websites in which some of these poems were previously published:
Haight Ashbury Literary Review, 2006, "Goodnight"
"Asakasa Mall"
Between the Fault Lines, 2013, Sugartown Publishing, "Angels", "Wood and Earth", "West Wind", "All for Yusef", "Writing Group"

New Sun Rising: Stories for Japan, *2012*, Raging Aardvark
Publishing, "Steps and Bows in Tokyo"
The Widows' Handbook: Poetic Reflections on Grief and Survival,
2014, Kent State University Press, "Ghosts I Have Met",
"Light Bulbs"
River of Earth and Sky: Poems for the Twenty-First Century, 2015,
"Angels", "Bee Story"
A Southern Sampler, 2013, Southern Sampler Artists Colony Press,
"Ghost Veils"
Turning a Train of Thought Upside Down, 2012, Scarlet Tanager
Press, "I Want to Dance", "Recycling"
Downdirtyword.com — *The Legendary, 2011*,
"My Scars are My Tattoos"
spectermagazine.com, 2012, "Dark Side of the Rainbow"
San Diego Poetry Annual 2014-2015, "To My Son"
The Scribbler, 2015, "Bite"

About the Author

Marianne Betterly is an award-winning poet who writes about nature, love, loss, the streets of San Francisco, fairy tales and the synchronicity of events. A believer in auguries, old and new, she loves to discover hidden meaning floating on a double latte, in a swarm of bees or in a murder of crows.

Her poetry has been published widely in books and journals including *River of Earth and Sky*, *The Widows' Handbook*, *Between the Fault Lines*, *Turning a Train of Thought Upside Down*, *The Legendary*, *New Sun Rising: Stories for Japan*, *Hot Flashes*, *Southern Sampler*, *Green Silk Journal*, *San Diego Poetry Annual 2014-15*, *Specter Magazine*, *San Diego Poetry Annual 2014-2015* and the *Haight Ashbury Literary Journal*. Marianne lives in a house in Kensington once owned by the great-nephew of Ralph Waldo Emerson.

www.ingramcontent.com/pod-product-compliance
Lightning Source LLC
Chambersburg PA
CBHW032022090426
42741CB00006B/707